Good for You!

MY FIRST MANNERS

Written by Catherine Lukas

Illustrated by Joel Schick

Published by Phoenix International Publications, Inc.
8501 West Higgins Road, Suite 300, Chicago, Illinois 60631
Lower Ground Floor, 59 Gloucester Place, London W1U 8JJ

www.pikidsmedia.com

p i kids is a trademark of Phoenix International Publications, Inc., and is registered in the United States.

8 7 6 5 4 3 2 1

ISBN: 978-1-4127-6786-6

phoenix international publications, inc.

"It's Guy Smiley here! Welcome to
Let's Try New Foods!
That's the game show where we ... try new foods."

"Cookie Monster has earned himself a point for being polite and trying squash!"

"All right, Elmo. What's our next food?"

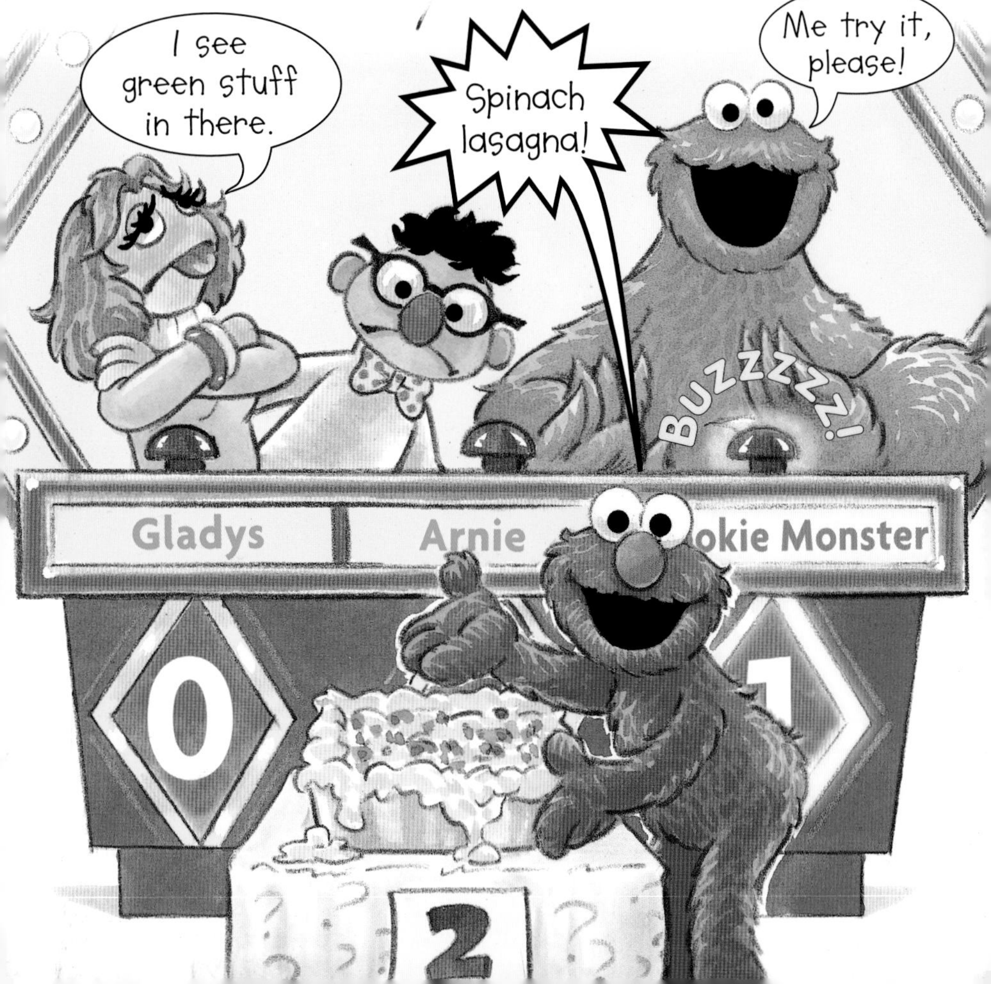

"Oh my, Cookie Monster certainly did not mind trying that good-for-you food!"

"That's it! That's the game! Cookie Monster is our big winner after tasting collard greens. Yay! Elmo, bring out the prize for our winner."

"Our lucky winner gets a set of pots and
pans to cook his own new foods!
What do you think, Cookie Monster?"